ENGLISH COSTUME OF
THE EIGHTEENTH CENTURY

1705

English Costume

of the

Eighteenth Century

Drawn by
IRIS BROOKE

Described by
JAMES LAVER

Adam and Charles Black

FIRST PUBLISHED 1931
REPRINTED 1945, 1950, 1958, 1964, 1970, 1977

A. & C. Black Ltd
35 Bedford Row, London wc1r 4jh
© a. & c. black ltd

isbn 0 7136 0158 2

PRINTED IN GREAT BRITAIN BY TINDAL PRESS LTD.

FOREWORD

THE phrase " eighteenth-century costume " is one dear
to theatrical costumiers, and (although there has been
a very considerable diffusion of knowledge during the last
few years) it is still too often used as though the same clothes
were worn from 1700 to 1800. Eighteenth-century plays
are frequently dressed quite regardless of changes in fashion
throughout the century. Ramillies wigs are wedded to
1790 hats ; Louis XV. petticoats are worn with the towering
head-dresses of 1770, and Watteau gowns are matched with
toilettes of the French Directory.

That there is some excuse for this the following pages
bear witness. There is indeed a singular homogeneity about
the period, and when one considers that fashions came in
and went out more slowly than they do at present, that the
difference between town and country was more marked, and
that old people clung more affectionately to the modes of
their youth, there is perhaps less absurdity in treating the
century as one than might at first appear.

The present editor would be the last person to advocate
a pedantic archæological accuracy in reconstructing the
costume and background of the Comedy of Manners. There
is a sense in which the eighteenth century—if we forget the
revolutionary fervour of its close—was static, as timeless
and changeless as a Platonic Idea. The three-cornered hat,
the Watteau gown, the wig, the snuff-box, the shoe-buckles,
the knee-breeches, and the sword at a man's side—these are
surely Types laid up in Heaven.

The sixteenth century had been convulsed by the Reforma-
tion, the seventeenth by the Wars of Religion ; all was
confusion, all was flux. But in the eighteenth century the
surface of civilisation seemed to have set hard ; a culture
had been evolved which, however incapable of satisfying the
eternal needs of man, was, of its kind, perfect and complete.

That is not to say that it had no hidden misery and horror, no filth, no squalor, no sordid poverty. It had all these things; but it had also a Society, in the true sense, a European Society conscious of its unity and its common culture, and able therefore to devote itself to the elaboration of the elegancies of life, in a word to the evolution of Style. In nearly all the countries of Europe, Aristocracy had come to terms with Monarchy and had not yet been overwhelmed by the democratic flood. *Après nous, le déluge!* But till it came, the polite world enjoyed itself, and has left to future ages a complete picture of a homogeneous culture, a culture in which formal religion was tempered by scepticism and extravagance was restrained by taste, and in which two arts at least were brought to their perfection: the art of letter-writing and the art of conversation.

The calm was, of course, delusive, the seemingly solid surface scored with fissures and threatened with subterranean upheaval. Every age, no matter how static it may appear, is an age of transition, and the eighteenth century was no exception. Thought changed and fashion with it, and the century which began with Addison ended by accepting the extravagances of Rousseau. Costume is not a triviality; it is the visible raiment of the soul. It is the purpose of the present book to display the slow but, in the end, considerable changes which affected European costume during the eighteenth century.

1700—1705

THE beginning of the century found the dress of Charles II.'s last years only slightly modified by the intervening reigns. James introduced no innovations, and the slight Dutch influence due to William III. only served to give to dress a certain stiffness and sombreness in keeping with the temperament of a King who cared nothing for the elegancies of life. Queen Anne, with whom the century opened, brought neither gaiety nor ostentation to a Court singularly lacking in both, and the dress of her period followed the rigid form of her predecessors. The main lines of costume, however, as it was to exist for nearly a century, were already decided, and this costume had certain strong characteristics which must be briefly considered.

The most remarkable of such characteristics is the wig. Wigs were worn in France very early in the seventeenth century, but did not reach England until the Restoration. Charles II. wore a voluminous black wig, and throughout his reign the wig fell on each side of the face with the ends drooping on to the chest. This proved so inconvenient, especially for soldiers, that the fashion arose of tying the hair back with a ribbon, and ultimately, of enclosing it at the back in a silk bag. But this, at the opening of the century, was still in the future. The cost of wigs was enormous, as much as £30 being frequently paid for a full wig of real hair. When one considers that this must be the equivalent of several hundred pounds of our money, it is not surprising that foot-pads should make a first snatch at their victims' wigs.

Men's coats were so long that they almost concealed the breeches, and the waistcoats were almost as long as the coats. Shoe-buckles came in with William III., and were at first very small. They soon grew larger, and were often ornamented with jewels.

Women's dress was somewhat severe, although it had certain elements of informality. The small laced apron was much worn, even on important occasions. Below it was the flowered petticoat, much more important than the skirt, which was frequently drawn back in bunches or folds. The bodice of the dress, although cut low, was very stiff.

1705—1710

THE most striking thing about female costume at the beginning of the eighteenth century was the height of the head-dress. The fashion started in France when Mademoiselle Fontange, the King's mistress, finding her hair disordered while out hunting, tied it up with a ribbon. The fashion was followed, and formalised, so that soon an elaborate high lace cap stood on the women's heads, the hair being piled up in front and adorned with a wire frame covered with lace and ribbons. The Fontange head-dress was called a " commode " in England, and was seen as early as the end of James II.'s reign. It lasted throughout the reign of William and Mary, and, at the accession of Queen Anne, rose even higher. The lace used was very costly, for there was as yet no substitute for the real lace of Brussels and Mechlin except gauze, which did not give the same effect.

Men's hair was cropped very close, and in private the heavy full-bottomed wig was frequently discarded, an embroidered cap being worn in its place. Poets and painters are frequently represented in this curious negligé Waistcoats were still excessively long, and had to be left unbuttoned at the bottom in order to allow freedom to the limbs. Shirts were made of fine white lawn, with elaborate lace frills down the front and at the wrists. The cravat, which was also of lace, was one of the most costly parts of the costume. The sword was, of course, worn by all gentlemen, and had not yet assumed the dainty proportions of the dress-sword later in the century—a sword of the same size and shape as that which survives to-day in Court dress. Small boys did not wear a wig, but kept their own hair long in a kind of curly mop.

1700—1710

THE neckcloth, or cravat, had been worn by German troops as early as 1640, and, soon after the beginning of the new century, began to replace the lace collar in general use. It consisted of a strip of white material about a foot wide and a yard long, twisted round the neck and knotted in front. Considerable variety was practised in the manner of tying it, and each variety had a special name. A Steinkerk was a lace cravat tied very loosely, with the ends passed through a buttonhole in the coat. It was so called after the Battle of Steinkerk, where the French officers went into action so hurriedly that they had not time to tie their cravats properly ; and the fashion was popular in England in spite of the fact that Steinkerk was an English defeat.

The large wig was worn by the wealthy, unconfined by any kind of ribbon or fastening, a fashion which must have been extremely inconvenient for those whose occupations involved rapid physical action.

The very short sleeve of Charles II.'s time had given place to a longer variety, with very elaborate turned-back cuffs, adorned with buttons and embroidery. Women's sleeves remained almost the same for many years. They were short, reaching to just below the elbow, and were finished with rather wide lace ruffles. Sometimes the lace was attached to the chemisette underneath, and not to the gown itself.

The odd habit of wearing patches on the face lasted almost throughout the century, and patches of different shapes and sizes were worn by women of all ages. Painting the face was freely indulged in, and the paints used sometimes contained chemicals very harmful to the complexion. The face was treated with wash-balls compounded of white lead, rice, and flour, with washes of quicksilver boiled in water, and with bismuth. This mattered less, perhaps, because women expected to look old in the early 'thirties.

1710

THERE is no very noticeable change in men's attire during the first ten years of the eighteenth century. Coats and waistcoats remained very long with large pockets in the flaps of each. The stockings were worn outside the breeches, drawn up over the knee, but gartered below. Stockings could be of coloured silk—blue or scarlet—with gold or silver clocks, but youths and poorer men wore black stockings of wool. In winter the curious fashion was followed of wearing several pairs of stockings at once.

In women's dress the fashions of the end of the previous century had been but slightly modified. The corset, which had reappeared about 1670, was worn very tight, and the bodice of the over-dress cut to fit exactly over it. It was laced from the bottom, with the effect of forcing the breasts upwards. Bodices were low, and a crimped frill was added to the upper edge—a survival from the lace collar of the previous age.

Already before the close of the seventeenth century gowns began to be looped up at the sides into *paniers*, and these *paniers* were superseded by hoops, which soon grew to enormous dimensions. The hoop was not, like the crinoline, an under-garment, but the outside petticoat itself stiffened with whalebone. The over-gown opened in front, and the petticoat was frequently of damask or other rich cloth. In winter petticoats were sometimes made of ermine, but, as by their nature, they were some little distance from the body of the wearer, they could not have made her much warmer. Petticoat, gown, stays, and cloak could be of different colours, but it was the petticoat which was usually embroidered and therefore formed the richest part of the toilet.

1710—1720

IN its earliest and most elaborate form the full-bottomed wig was divided into three masses of curls, two in front of the shoulders and one hanging down the back. Above the forehead the hair rose into two peaks or horns, sometimes exaggerated to grotesque proportions. However, the fashion served to give increased height to the figure, and a grave dignity to the face. A hat was completely unnecessary, and was often carried in the hand, but when worn, had to be of considerable size. The back of the head was smooth, the artificial curls forming a fringe at the edge of the wig.

The hoop petticoat made its first appearance in the London streets in 1711, and two English ladies, walking in the gardens of the Tuileries in 1718, set the fashion in France. It has been suggested that it came from Germany, from some little Court where the great wheel farthingale known to Queen Elizabeth and to Anne of Denmark had survived for more than a century. The revived hoop was at its biggest in England at the end of the other Queen Anne's reign.

The skirts of a man's coat were stiffened with wire to make them stand out, but men soon abandoned the attempt to compete with their wives in this particular.

Falbalas came in early in the century. These were crimped or pleated flounces sewn horizontally round the skirt, and were sometimes of a different material. This was not true of *volants* or wide ruffles, which were assumed to be part of the original dress.

The English corset was in general laced at the back, and the whalebone stiffening went right round the body and across the breast. The top edge was stiffened with a stout wire, and in the lining in front a small pocket was contrived to hold satchets of fragrant herbs. The French corset continued to be laced up the front.

1715

IT is often assumed that dress in the eighteenth century was very much more formal than it is to-day. In reality it was much less so, in the sense that considerably greater variety was permitted to individual taste, and that costume had not yet crystallised, as it were, into various accepted forms for different occasions and different occupations. An eighteenth-century gentleman would have been astonished at the uniformity of men's evening-dress, and even at the comparative uniformity of their everyday attire. Pages were not yet dressed in buttons, nor Eton boys in short coats and white collars. If lawyers wore full-bottomed wigs, so did every other dignified man. Lackeys wore the costume of the day with certain modifications ; there was even a certain amount of liberty allowed in officers' uniforms, and a definitely naval costume had not yet been invented. In particular, Court dress was simply the dress of the day, a little more elaborate and a little more costly.

Immense numbers of diamonds were worn both by men and women, for since the Dutch improvements in diamond-cutting at the beginning of the century, the stones could be made to present a much more brilliant effect than formerly. Diamonds were often borrowed or even hired for important occasions, such as Courts and weddings. The somewhat rigid bodice-fronts of this period lent themselves to the display of precious stones, and the stomacher was frequently embroidered all over with them, or else heavily laced with gold thread. Peers and Knights of the Garter and other orders wore their decorations even in the street, so that a man's rank could be easily recognised. We are still far from the days when it is considered bad form to wear even a miniature military ribbon. In this sense the dress of the eighteenth century was very formal ; and although the middle classes tried to ape the nobility, the high cost of the materials worn compelled them to keep at a respectful distance.

1710—1720

THE fashion for wearing the full-bottomed wig divided into three masses of curls did not last very long, owing to the growing consciousness of its inconvenience, even among the leisured.   Later, the wig was of equal length all round, but sometimes the portion at the back was divided into two, the ends being tied with ribbons.   This fashion persisted among old men until about 1760, but in general wigs became smaller about 1720, and continued to diminish in size throughout the century.

Cuffs were still large and sometimes heavily embroidered, but disappeared from hunting and riding coats.   Riding was also responsible for a modification of the coat-tails. These were buttoned back, and soon became merely orna-mental, *i.e.* the revers were formalised as part of the decora-tion of the coat, thus making the wider opening at the front of the coat permanent.   The last vestige of this buttoning back is to be seen in the two black buttons in the small of the back of a modern morning or evening coat and in the more elaborate arrangement of buttons on the back lower edge of a soldier's tunic.

The most notable change in female attire is a lowering of the head-dress.   On the disappearance of the " commode " or Fontange head-dress, the hair was worn in a simple, almost negligent style, rather close to the head.   This fashion lasted, with but slight modifications, until the introduction of the towering head-dresses typical of the seventeen-seventies.   The habit of wearing caps, however, persisted, particularly in the middle classes.   These caps were usually quite small and perched on the top of the head, but were sometimes very rich, trimmed with fine lace, or made of lace entirely.   Servants' caps, or the caps worn by very old ladies and peasant women, are now the only survivals of this practice.

1720

A T the beginning of the century the increased facilities for trade with the East, due to the growing success of the East India Company, led to the introduction of vast quantities of Indian calicoes, which soon became very popular. English cloth manufacturers grew alarmed, and Acts of Parliament were passed, both by Queen Anne and George I., prohibiting the use of calicoes, silks, etc., from India, Persia, and China. These were, however, extensively smuggled, and Steele, in his plea for the weavers of England, gives an interesting list of the materials they had displaced : brilliants, pulerays, antherines, bombazines, satinets, chiverets, ora-guellas, grazetts (flowered and plain), footworks, coloured crapes (although most crape was made in Italy and was regarded by rigid Protestants as Popish), damasks, and worsted tammy draughts.

A wide over-dress came into fashion about this period. It hung loose from the shoulders and could be fastened down the front with bows of ribbon. This, which was called a *contouche*, was the equivalent of the modern *peignoir*, and at first was worn only in the house as a morning-dress, but soon became so popular that it appeared everywhere in the street. It could be made of silk, wool, or taffeta and sometimes of light materials, such as gauze or muslin, worn over an under-dress of a contrasting colour. Its effect was one of charming negligence in attire, and is typical of the change which was taking place, less noticeably in England than in France, from the stiff formalism of the age of Louis XIV. to the rather frivolous elegance of the Rococo period. Men's coats were still rather sombre in hue, embroidery being reserved for the decoration of the waistcoat, which was often the most valuable part of the costume, unless the lace ruffles of the shirt were exceptionally fine.

1720—1725

THE seventeen-twenties were marked by the increasing popularity of the *contouche*, already described. It must not be thought, however, that the wearing of one of these loose dresses meant the abandonment of corsets. These formed an essential part of the under-dress, and were still worn very tightly laced in order to give a small waist to the figure, even when this was completely hidden by the full *contouche*.

Until about the year 1725, men wore on the right shoulders of their coats a number of bows of ribbon, the long ends of which extended to the elbows. These were a relic of the shoulder fastening which had been used at the end of the seventeenth century to secure the sword belt. Swords were now worn less conspicuously and sometimes discarded altogether except on formal occasions or for going about London by night, when the unarmed pedestrian was at the mercy of footpads and riotous marauders of all kinds. It was usual, therefore, to go to evening entertainments in the company of friends or servants.

Heel-making was a separate trade, employing a large number of hands, and this fact no doubt contributed to the persistence of high heels. The heels even of men's shoes were in general high, those of women extremely so. They were made of wood and coloured. In France, red heels were a sign of noble birth. The shape of shoes in general, even women's shoes, was somewhat clumsy, the heels being far too small and placed too near the middle of the instep. It would have been impossible to walk far in such shoes, and in the house women wore slippers.

For out of doors, ladies wore a long cloak with a hood attached to it. It was originally of scarlet cloth, and perhaps for that reason was called a " cardinal." It remained scarlet until the close of the century, when it became the fashion to wear black cloaks. It is interesting to note that the "cardinal" was the cloak worn by "Little Red Riding Hood " in the nursery story.

1725—1730

TRAVELLING cloaks for men were long and circular
in shape, in fact they differed little from the *chlamys*
of the Greeks (except that this was oblong), or the cloaks
worn by Spanish peasants to this day.   The appalling state
of the roads in wet weather made high, stout boots essential,
and these were of the pattern familiar from pictures of the
Restoration period but with narrower tops, and, of course,
unadorned with lace round the upper edge.   For riding
and travelling, women wore a modification of the male
coat with turned-back sleeves and cravat, but their skirts
were ill-adapted for any kind of exercise.

By 1730 the re-introduced farthingale may be said to have
established itself, to last, with slight modifications, until the
French Revolution.   It grew to six feet in diameter and
required an enormous quantity of stuff to cover it.   At
first, hoops of osier rods or cane were used, but these were
superseded by the more reliable whalebone.   The hoop was
at first simply a cage—a series of hoops of different dimensions attached to one another by ribbons or strings at intervals
round their circumference.   About 1729 it became customary
to cover this cage with cloth, with taffeta, and finally with
silk, so that the hoop became a reinforced skirt.   Sometimes in summer no other skirt was worn, and as the wearing
of drawers was still very uncommon, the limbs were naked
underneath the hoop except for the stockings which reached
to just above the knee and were fastened by garters just
below it.   Hoops were violently denounced from the pulpit,
but from any contest with the clergy fashion has always
emerged victorious, and they continued to be worn even by
servant girls, and by countrywomen going to market.   Even
the simplest *négligé* was duly provided with its framework of
whalebone, and it became impossible for two women to
walk abreast in the narrow streets or to occupy a carriage
together in comfort.   Even the staircases in private houses
had to be provided with balusters curved outward in order
to allow for the passage of the voluminous skirts.

1720—1730

BAG-WIGS were at first worn chiefly by soldiers, and when they made their way into civilian costume were regarded, in the beginning, as a kind of undress. The bag was made of gummed black taffeta, with a bow of the same material, and served to give an appearance of neatness without much trouble. The pig-tail was almost as popular as the bag-wig and for the same reasons of convenience. The *toupet*, or hair immediately over the forehead, was often natural, the join between the wig and the real hair being disguised by a liberal use of powder.

About 1730 the fashion arose of leaving the top buttons of the waistcoat unfastened in order to display the elaborately frilled shirt. This led to a modification of the neckcloth, which had shorter ends in order that the decorated shirt-front might be more easily seen. Sometimes the cravat with shorter ends was replaced by a neckcloth knotted at the back and kept in place in front by a jewelled pin. Military men wore two neckcloths one over the other, the under one of white muslin and that over it of coloured silk, allowing the white of the first to show between the folds.

Throughout the century, women's sleeves were almost constant in length, that is to say, the material of the dress reached just to the point of the elbow, and further length was given by two or three frills of lace. Although the elaborate " commode " had disappeared, smaller caps of lace were still worn in the house by women of all ranks and all ages. The styles of hairdressing varied considerably but within narrow limits, the hair being kept fairly close to the head. The necks of dresses were worn very low, in fact as low as a modern evening-dress, except that the opening was not so deep at the back.

1730

THE three-cornered hat, than which nothing is more typical of eighteenth-century fashion, was capable of a considerable amount of variety. Some hats were still laced and garnished with plumes like those of the previous epoch, but as the plume was worn on the upper brim, now bent inwards, it only appeared as a kind of fringe. Some hats were simply bordered with braid. The triangular form was kept by means of a cord, passed through holes in the brim and drawn tight round the crown, or else by a button acting as a kind of clip at the edge of the upturned brim. The earlier habit of festooning the hat with ribbons had been definitely abandoned.

The accession of George II. made very little difference to costume in England. The new king, like the old, was German, stiff in his manners and somewhat slovenly in his habits. His Court provided no centre of influence for the caprices of Society or the whims of fashion. Individual members of the aristocracy wielded far more influence than the Royal Family, and those who could afford trips to the Continent became, by natural consequence, the arbiters of taste.

Two accessories of costume in constant use were the snuff-box and the fan. The first was carried by every man, of every degree, and by many ladies. The smoking of tobacco was considered definitely " low," to be practised only by sailors and labourers, but vast quantities of the weed were consumed in the form of snuff powder, and every elegance of decoration was bestowed upon the boxes in which it was carried.

The fan was universal. In Queen Anne's reign it had been very large. Later, it became less pretentious and was decorated with painted scenes by the most able artists. Sometimes the paintings were designed to show political opinions. The material used was paper or, sometimes, thin white chicken skin, and the handles could be ornamented with jewels or enamels.

1730—1735

IN 1734 women's stays were worn extremely low. The bodies of gowns were laced up the front over a stomacher, or else stays were worn outside ; but in general there is little change in feminine costume since the last decade.

Men's costume also remained almost static, although the bag-wig was steadily ousting more elaborate types of coiffure. The turned back cuffs, frequently of contrasting colour to that of the coat, were cut in " pagoda " fashion, that is to say, narrow at the wrist and expanding sharply along the forearm. The name is a sufficient indication of the slight Oriental influence which made itself felt throughout the eighteenth century, not, however, so much affecting the shape of clothes as their colour, material, and decoration.

In France about 1730 men began to fasten their breeches at the knee over the stockings, but the older mode persisted among Englishmen for some years longer. The winter of 1729 was one of exceptional severity, and fine gentlemen, finding their thin stockings an insufficient protection against the cold, wore for a few months a kind of military gaiter. Men of the lower classes, with their grey or black woollen stockings, were better protected and had no need to adopt this short-lived fashion.

The fashion of leaving the waistcoat open in front in order to display the linen has been already mentioned. The custom reached its extreme in the early 'thirties. Sometimes, about a foot of frilled shirt was shown—a fashion to which the modern dress shirt and low-cut waistcoat can be ultimately traced. Women's riding-habits affected, as so often, a masculine mode, the waistcoat being shorter but of the same pattern, and the hat smaller but similar in shape to those worn by men.

Men's pockets were very ample and the folds of the long coat made it possible to carry comparatively bulky objects in them without spoiling their shape. Some fashionable gentlemen would carry a whole battery of snuff-boxes in the skirts of their coats.

1735—1740

THE arrival of Queen Caroline in England (for previously
the Royal Court had remained in Hanover) gave a
certain impulse to fashion, which had for some time languished
without a leader. The Queen of George II. had a great
liking for flowered silks, usually with a white ground em-
bossed all over with a large pattern of gold, silver, or colours.

George II. himself had no pretensions to be a leader of
fashion. His tastes were those of a simple soldier, and he
had no feeling for any of the elegances of life. The ladies
he honoured with his favour were neither beautiful nor
elegant, and the English aristocracy went its own way, in-
dependent of the Court, adopting French fashions to its own
slightly more rural use, but inventing little of its own. The
prestige which English costume was to exercise all over the
Continent was still more than half a century in the future.

Women of the middle classes still dressed with a certain
austerity, although the wives and daughters of rich City
merchants did their best to copy the fashions of St. James's.
Some of the merchants themselves assumed, on Sundays, the
fine coats and elaborate periwigs of the nobility.

Women's stockings, until the middle of the seventeen-
thirties, were of all colours, green being one of the favourites.
They were worked with clocks of gold, silver, or coloured
silks. About 1737, however, there was a sudden rage for
white stockings which greatly alarmed contemporary
moralists. White stockings seemed to the preachers little
better than nudity, but they continued to be worn until
almost the end of the century. As a matter of fact very
little of the stocking was seen, as dresses were never shorter
in this period than to just above the ankles. Dancing or
climbing into a coach may have revealed a certain amount
of stocking to the eyes of the curious, but not enough, one
would have thought, to alarm the most rigorous censor of
morals.

1730—1740

IN addition to tie-wigs of many varieties there appeared, in the reign of George II., bob-wigs of various kinds. These imitated natural hair much more closely than the grand peruques; they were worn by professional men, citizens, and even by apprentices; lawyers affected a high frontlet and a long bag at the back tied in the middle, undergraduates a wig with a flat top to allow for the academic cap.

Cravats in this period show very few modifications; in fact, although there were many varieties, each variety was almost as static as the modern neck-tie. The fronts and cuffs of shirts continued to be elaborately frilled. Coat-cuffs were wide and deep and sometimes heavily embroidered with silk flowers or with patterns in gold and silver thread.

There is little change to record in the forms of women's head-dresses. The ideal of the small, neat head was maintained; caps became even smaller than they had been, and curls more neatly trimmed and arranged. The general shape of the female figure continued to be an equilateral triangle, resting securely on a wide base. The lower part of the body was inside the skirt rather than clothed by it, the only underclothes worn being in the form of a long " smock " or chemise. The evolution of underclothes should form an interesting and necessary chapter in the history of fashion. The phrase " body-linen " is still sometimes used, but actual linen underclothes must now be extremely rare. In the eighteenth century, however, linen was the usual material, very fine Dutch linen being imported for ladies' " smocks." Scotch or Irish linen could be bought for a third of the price, but was coarser and not so highly esteemed. Silk and lace-trimmed underwear was unknown in the eighteenth century.

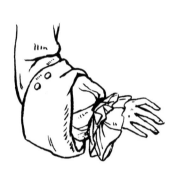

1740

THE inconvenience of the circular hoop led to the introduction of one oval in shape, and much more graceful
in appearance. The materials, although not so heavy as
the brocades used early in the century, were very rich, and
often extremely costly.

An ingenious method was evolved (or rather revived
from the Elizabethan and Caroline periods) for decorating
women's dresses. This was the process of quilting which
had the added advantage, in winter, of making the clothes
much warmer. A layer of wadding was spread between
the lining (which had to be of linen or some equally strong
material) and the material of the dress, and was kept in
place by an elaborate stitchery pattern. Another method of
decoration was to cut out shapes of the same material as the
dress and to sew them on to it, having first inserted a stuffing
of wadding. These were known as " plastic ornaments."

As the century advanced, and the general prosperity increased, there was a gradual filtering down of luxury from
the aristocracy to the upper middle-classes. Working
people, especially in the large towns, often lived under
conditions which would not now be tolerated, but the
general standard of life rose steadily, until the set-back of the
Industrial Revolution.

The fine ladies of the period vied in extravagance with
their sisters on the other side of the Channel, and like them
adopted certain exotic modes intended to give them an air
of elegant eccentricity. The possession of a monkey or a
green parrot was a sign of luxurious refinement, and those
who could afford it went even further and purchased a little
black boy as a personal attendant. The presence of such a
slave, dressed in bright coloured and fantastic clothes, was
eminently calculated to set off both the toilette and the white
skin of his mistress.

1740—1745

IT should not be forgotten, in considering the costumes of a period as remote from us as the eighteenth century, that the tyranny of fashion was nothing like so complete as it is at present. Perhaps it would be truer to say that although fashion was tyrannical it was much less swift in its operation and, in the absence of fashion plates, a change in dress took much longer to filter down through the different strata of society. People in the country might well be twenty years behind the fashion, and the older men and women, even in towns, sometimes did not trouble to adjust themselves to changing taste.

In 1740, for example, it was quite possible to see an oldish man walking, even in the fashionable St. James's Park, in a large full-bottomed wig, while his son beside him wore one much smaller and neater. Older men clung also to their old-fashioned cravats, just as older men to-day wear the collars which were usual in their youth. There is perhaps no article of a man's attire about which he seems so conservative as his neckwear.

Women's dress shows certain modifications which must be briefly noted. The *sacque* gown, hanging loose from the shoulders and gathered in great folds over the hooped petticoat, appeared in 1740. It was another example of the general tendency to exalt the *négligé* into general wear. The effect could be charming, but involved considerable skill in dressmaking. Examination of the actual dresses of the period reveals the delicate cutting which was necessary in order to give the loose appearance at the back and yet mould the dress to the figure, for the falling folds were not added afterwards like a cape, but were an essential part of the back of the bodice.

c

1745—1750

THE loose *contouche*, already described, went out of fashion at the end of the seventeen-forties. Instead, there was introduced a gown or *robe ronde*, which opened from the waist downwards to display an underdress of the same material. In morning attire the place of the *contouche* was taken by various kinds of powder-mantles or dressing-jackets. The practice of powdering the hair demanded some kind of protection for the dress while the operation was being performed, and the toilette of a fashionable lady took up so much of her time and was attended, as a kind of informal reception, by so many of her friends (particularly men), that some kind of garment was necessary which was both warm and becoming. A woman of fashion was surrounded, from the moment she got out of bed, by a crowd of admirers, dressmakers, furniture vendors, musicians, dancing-masters, and dependents. Such a miniature court can be studied in all its detail in the well-known engraving by Hogarth.

Women's shoes were excessively flimsy and ill-adapted to any kind of hard wear. This fact receives interesting confirmation from a document, found among Lady Suffolk's papers, which gives details of the dress allowances for the daughters of George II. The provision was not on the whole extravagant, twelve pairs of thread stockings and two dozen cambric pocket-handkerchiefs being expected to last for two years, but a new pair of shoes, at six shillings a pair, was provided every week. Nine " day shifts " and nine " night shifts " were given to the princesses yearly, but the allowance of gloves rose to the astonishing annual figure of sixteen dozen pairs. It must be remembered, however, that in Royal households servants rapidly acquire a right to certain perquisites, and that articles of clothing were given away long before they were worn out. It was enacted, however, that the fine lace trimmings on the princesses' garments were not to be given away but saved for future use.

1740—1750

IN the early 'forties of the eighteenth century wigs became somewhat smaller, sometimes not touching the shoulders at all. By dandies they were sometimes worn exceedingly small, although satirical prints of the period probably over-stressed their minuteness. The hat became smaller also, with very little border turned up to make the three-cornered shape. Cravats were smaller, and as this exposed more of the shirt, the front of this was more extravagantly frilled. The turned-down collar of the coat made an occasional appearance, as if in anticipation of the fashions at the end of the century, but this was unusual in the 'forties. Cuffs were still large but tended to be somewhat narrower at the wrist. Later in the decade hats were larger again, but wigs remained small, a contrast which had the effect of making the hat seem larger still.

Women still wore their hair somewhat close to the head, with one or two curls falling behind and others encircling the face. Caps were universally worn, sometimes approximating in shape to those worn by Mary, Queen of Scots, a lady to whom fashion has more than once returned for fresh inspiration. " Milkmaid " fashions for women had already made their appearance, and these involved country hats tied negligently under the chin with ribbons. Such hats are the remote ancestors of the nineteenth-century poke-bonnet. Throughout the eighteenth century colours had a political significance, and it is interesting to note that white hat-ribbons at this period denoted Jacobite sympathies. It is not always realised how much sympathy there was in England in 1745 for the attempt of the Young Pretender on the throne of his ancestors. If he had succeeded, the formalising influence of a German Court would have been removed, and English fashions would have been rapidly assimilated to those of the French, as had happened once before on the Restoration of another Charles Stuart.

1750

THE middle of the century marked what is perhaps the highest point of rococo style. The stiffness of the earlier years had been abandoned, and the extravagances of the 'seventies and the neo-classical negligence of the 'nineties were alike unthought of. The most typical characteristics of the century were at their most charming stage. The wig was neat and becoming. The three-cornered hat was of medium size—it had been ridiculously large in Marlborough's time, and became ridiculously small in 1790 ; coats and waist-coats were both dignified and graceful, the cut was good and the embroidery elegant. There was a tasteful moderation in the use of lace.

Women's dress was marked by a peculiarly charming form of the side *panier*, and was made of bright stuffs not too rich and heavy, for one result of the large *panier* had been to lead to the introduction of lighter and more flexible materials for dresses. In the late seventeenth and early eighteenth centuries very heavy stuffs had been worn, as these lent themselves to the somewhat rigid silhouettes of fashionable costume. The feminine frame, while capable of much in deference to fashion, cannot support an unlimited quantity of heavy brocade interwoven with metal strands. Some women managed to support damask, which is a heavy material, but looked well, with its bold patterns, when stretched over hoops ; but for the majority the result of the new modes was the introduction of lawn, muslin, and dimity, of simple texture but lively pattern, little bouquets or scattered flowers being the most frequent. The universal crinoline of a century later was to have a very similar effect.

1750—1755

THE year 1750 witnessed a striking decrease in the size of hoops, but the fashion for widening the skirt by the artificial aid of whalebone or osier rods was not to be abandoned for another generation, and in Court dress for another sixty years. The persistence and recurrence of hoops is one of the oddest phenomena in the history of fashion, and it is by no means absolutely certain, even yet, that they will not return. In 1800 it may well have seemed that they had gone for ever, but they had assumed their most extravagant form again in 1860, and that in the middle of the triumphs of the machine age, when the necessity of getting in and out of railway carriages might well seem to have made their use impossible.

Tight-lacing also, prevalent in 1750, was equally so a century later, and may come in again unless it is defeated by the modern enthusiasm for sport. Although it is always dangerous to generalise in questions of fashion, it may be said that tight-lacing is never very far away when the waist-line is normal. The only way to be certain of abolishing the corset is to push the waistline to just below the breasts, as was done during the first decade of the nineteenth century, or to lower it to the hips, as was the fashion about 1928.

The fullness of women's dresses during the early seven-teen-fifties was reflected in the fullness of the skirts of men's coats. These, too, were sometimes stiffened with whale-bone, or at least kept in place by pads, an odd example of the rare influence of feminine on masculine modes, since no man wishes to give the appearance of having full hips. In general, masculine fashions influence those of women far more frequently than feminine fashions influence those of men.

1755—1760

CONTRARY to the fashion at the beginning of the century, men's suits were sometimes made of the same elaborately patterned material throughout. This could be a cut velvet or an embroidered silk, and was naturally costly. The silk embroidery on men's coats sometimes involved months or even years of labour on the part of embroideresses, whose skill and taste have never been surpassed. Embroidered waistcoats were often the work of a man's wife or daughters, and making them served to pass the long winter evenings in an age almost devoid of outside entertainment.

Women's dresses were also sometimes embroidered, but relied more often on a woven pattern, or on tucks and flounces in the material itself. In the actual form of dress there was very little change, and in England at least, in the last few years of the reign of George II., there was no very outstanding example of feminine elegance to give a lead to fashion. What tendency may be traced was rather in the direction of simplicity, or what passed for such in an essentially artificial age when women took no exercise beyond a quiet stroll. Some gowns affected an air of elegant negligence by having neither bodice nor girdle, but hanging loose from the shoulders over the wide *panier* ; others were fitted to the figure in front, but hung loose at the back. For this fashion heavy stuffs were unsuitable, so that dresses came to be made of lighter fabrics, such as lawn, muslin, or dimity, sometimes richly patterned, a tendency already noted as being due, in part, to the width of the hoops. The delicacy of the materials of dresses made some kind of protection from the weather doubly necessary. Cloaks with hoods were worn, and the sedan chair, for those who could afford it, saved the shoes of the ladies from being spoilt by the appallingly muddy streets. It is worthy of note that the umbrella first made its appearance in the London streets in 1756. It was carried by the philanthropist, Jonas Hanway, but his example was not generally followed for many years.

1750—1760

THE seventeen-fifties were a period of great importance in English history, and it is strange that the enormous military activity of the decade all over the world should have had so little effect even upon masculine fashions. The explanation, no doubt, lies partly in the fact that British victories took place for the most part in distant lands—at Plassey and at Quebec. Even the wars in Germany must have seemed sufficiently remote in that slow-travelling century, and although London swarmed with military men, especially in winter when the armies went into quarters, male fashion reflected the prevailing martial atmosphere only so far as to simplify the wig a little or give a military cock to the three-cornered hat.

On feminine costume the wars, unlike those of the Napoleonic era, left almost no trace at all, for the fashions were essentially feminine and so less susceptible than the revolutionary modes of the end of the century. It must also be remembered that the dress of soldiers was much closer in cut to that of civilians than during the days of the French Empire, when the fancy of military tailors was given full scope and the cut of uniforms decided for more than a century. Soldiers, in general, wore the civilian three-cornered hat, except that it was braided in a special way. Only grenadiers wore the mitre cap, and this was unlikely to be adopted for ordinary attire. The prevailing colour of British uniforms was already red, but the coats of civilians were frequently red also, and could be any colour. An officer was recognisable as such, but was by no means so conspicuous a figure in an ordinary crowd as a guardsman in full uniform would be to-day.

1760

A T the accession of George III., costume was, on the whole, simple, and the staid example of the Court did not tend to extravagance in dress. Hoops were still in use, but were of more reasonable size than had been fashionable a few years earlier. The small " gypsy hat " was worn even by the nobility. The gown was long-waisted and laced over the stomacher. Sleeves reached to the elbow, but full ruffles made them seem longer. Lace, in fact, was the chief extravagance, even the apron being frequently garnished with it. Handkerchiefs were frequently very costly, and more attention was paid to underclothes than during previous periods. Stockings were often white and made of silk and were fastened by garters, in general tied below the knee. Suspenders were, of course, impossible, as there was nothing to attach them to.

A *coqueluchon*, or small cape, covered the shoulders—a very necessary protection in cold weather, as bodices were somewhat low. Indeed, the high-necked bodice, even for day wear, is unusual until well on into the nineteenth century.

Children's costume, as such, had not yet been evolved, and boys and girls wore, with slight modification, replicas of their parents' clothes. Little girls, by modern standards, were far too heavily clad, and active boys were encumbered with long coats and three-cornered hats. In general, however, the costume of children showed, even as early as 1760, a tendency to simplicity and an adaptation to country usages, which gives it the appearance of anticipating the adult modes of the later century.

There is little hint in 1760 of the outbreak of fantasy in hairdressing which was to take place before the end of the decade.

1760—1765

THE end of the Seven Years' War made social inter-
course with France once more possible, and the
influence of French modes was suddenly renewed.   French
hairdressers, milliners, and modistes arrived in London in
considerable numbers and found ready patrons among the
wealthy English aristocracy.   Englishmen and women began
to pay visits to Paris and to bring new fashions with them
on their return.

Among other novelties was an adjustable farthingale.
This was an arrangement of hoops, or rather of iron ribs
encased in leather, and extending sideways from the waist
of the wearer in such a way that they could be raised at will.
In their normal position they extended horizontally outwards, the material of the dress hanging straight from them
to the ground, with the result that the skirt (if so monstrous
an object can be called a skirt), presented an oblong outline,
broader than it was high.   The ingenuity of the new arrangement lay in the fact that the main bars of the structure were
hinged at the wearer's waist, so that the whole apparatus
could be raised at each side like the two halves of the Tower
Bridge, and so make it possible to pass through doorways
and narrow lanes.   A modification of this fashion persisted, in
Court dress, into the nineteenth century.

Waists were very tight and long, with a pointed bodice,
often of satin, and cut very low.   To protect the chest from
cold, a " breast-front " of lace and ribbons was worn, but
even with this, women's dress, even in the daytime, presented an aspect of *décolletage* somewhat startling to modern
notions.   In winter small capes were worn as well as all-
enveloping cloaks, and in the early seventeen-sixties small
feather muffs were popular, both with men and women.
For the woman the muff also served in place of the as yet
uninvented handbag.   When muffs grew larger people were
in the habit of carrying small pet dogs in them.

1765—1770

THE second half of the seventeen-sixties was a period of tranquil prosperity for England. The Indian and Canadian conquests had swollen the Empire to proportions undreamed of in an earlier age. The English colonies in North America, although restive, had not yet broken away, and the British fleet was supreme in the waters of the world. An enormous increase in commerce resulted, affecting fashion by the importation of foreign, especially Oriental, stuffs, and also by the new wealth, not only of the London merchants, but of the lately-arisen race of those who had made licit or illicit fortunes under the none-too-strict surveillance of the East India Company.

The current variations of fashion may be briefly noted. " Hats," says a contemporary writer in *The London Chronicle,* " are now worn upon an average six inches and three-fifths broad in the brim and cocked between Quaker and Kevenhuller (*i.e.* the brims neither very loosely nor very closely attached to the crown). Some have their hats open before like a church spout . . . some wear them rather sharper like the nose of a greyhound. . . . There is a military cock and a mercantile cock, and while the beaux of St. James's wear their hats under their arms, the beaux of Moorfields all wear theirs diagonally over the left or right eye ; sailors wear their hats tucked uniformly down to the crown, and look as if they carried a triangular apple-pasty upon their heads."

The feminine coiffure, having been about the same for half a century, began to show signs of impending change. Already at the end of the seventeen-sixties woman had begun to abandon the small " head " and to pile the hair up from the forehead, in anticipation of the extravagant modes of the middle 'seventies. It was a definite breaking away from the close, simple hairdressing which had reigned supreme ever since the abandonment of the high Fontange or " commode " of lace and ribbon.

D

1760—1770

AS early as 1763 the Master Peruke Makers of London presented a petition to George III. in which they complained that gentlemen had begun to wear their own hair. The petition was without effect, for fashion is a heartless goddess and cares not how many honest tradesmen are ruined by her caprices. But the tendency was as yet little more than a tendency, and wigs continued to be worn by almost every man of any social pretensions for a generation longer. In 1770 there was a temporary fashion for round hats, forecasting the mode of the end of the century when the *tricorne* was definitely abandoned.

Innumerable varieties of neck-cloths were worn simultaneously, and there is little to add to what has already been said on the subject. Just as to-day one may see the " butter-fly " collar, the " turn-down " collar, and the soft collar which is derived from it, wedded to bows and ties, so in the period 1760 to 1770 contemporaries were wearing lace cravats, neck-cloths fastening at the back, and the black ribbon " solitaire " fastened in front with a jewelled pin.

The three sleeves illustrated on the opposite page show varying degrees of elaboration but with an undoubted trend towards simplicity and the ultimate adoption of a purely formal turn-back of the cuff.

In 1760 powder was still worn, but women's hair was dressed rather simply, sometimes being drawn back from the face *à la Chinoise*, and surmounted by a small knot of coloured silk ribbon. Round the throat could be worn a ruche of the same material as the dress, and a fichu was draped across the shoulders not only for warmth, but as a necessary article of dress, for bodices were sometimes cut so low as to be hardly decent. Some kind of cap was almost universally worn, and could either envelop the whole head like a hood, surround the face with a fringe of lace, or rest daintily on the top of the coiffure.

1770

THE remarkable feature of the 'seventies of the eighteenth century was the size of women's head-dresses. The change had begun in the late 'sixties, from the " snug " hairdressing of the previous decade to veritable mountains of frizz, stretched over wire frames and sometimes surmounted by fantastic structures resembling ships or windmills or gardens. As few ladies had sufficient hair of their own to comply with the new fashion, false locks were added, wool was used to fill up the interstices, and the whole was then liberally greased with pomatum and heavily dusted with white or grey powder. The dressing of such " heads " was an elaborate and costly business, so elaborate and costly that ladies of limited means had the operation performed as seldom as possible, with horribly unhygienic results.

For men, the bag-wig was very fashionable, and round the throat, the solitaire, in place of a cravat, was increasingly popular. Dandies (although the name, if not the thing itself, is an anachronism) wore flower buttonholes, often of roses, renewed every morning, like the orchid of Joseph Chamberlain in a later age. The coat-cuffs were embroidered, and the buckles of the shoe set with precious stones or paste. The colours of men's clothes were brighter than they had been earlier in the century, but simpler in cut, with shorter waistcoats and tail-coats tending somewhat to the shape of the " cut-away." Coats for formal wear were elaborately and often beautifully embroidered, with sprays of silk thread flowers on the cuffs, round the seams, and on the tails. Buttonholes became formalised, and collars were heavily decorated with needlework. Lace, however, was less in evidence as the century advanced, and as sleeves became longer and tighter there was less opportunity for its display.

1770—1775

CLOSE caps, resembling night-caps, were much worn in 1773, even in fashionable circles. Sometimes they had lace " wings " at the sides, giving a somewhat grotesque appearance to the head when seen from behind.

For a very short period men attempted to vie with women in the height of their head-dresses. The wig was built up with the aid of padding, or else rose steeply from the forehead in a kind of exaggerated *toupet*, with or without the support of a wire frame. As at the very beginning of the century when the full-bottomed wig had assumed such enormous proportions, it was now almost impossible for hats to be worn. The solution of the problem, however, was not, as it had been, to make the hat larger. On the contrary it became even smaller, and was never worn at all but merely carried in the hand and placed under the arm. Indeed, in polite society it became the masculine equivalent of the feminine fan.

This appurtenance of the toilet played a great part in eighteenth-century life. The rigid fan of the sixteenth century was an awkward engine compared with the graceful folding fan of the eighteenth. It could be carried easily, expanded quickly, and used both for cooling the face in the terribly overheated ballrooms of the period, and as an instrument of coquetry to add piquancy to smiling eyes, to conceal a blush, or to stifle a yawn. The mere fact that it could be folded within bone or ivory handles made it possible to use delicate materials such as silk or chicken-skin parchment, and to employ the best artists to paint exquisite little scenes thereon. Sometimes the fan, like the snuff-box, had a proper and a " gallant " side, either of which could be turned outwards at the will of the user. Some of the eighteenth-century fans which have come down to us are miracles of a delicate artistry which has never been surpassed.

1775—1780

THE head-dress of women reached its most fantastic height in the middle 'seventies; indeed, it almost seems as if the growing tendency for men to wear their own hair, or at least to combine more and more of their own hair with a diminishing wig, spurred the perruquiers on to invent even more elaborate head-dresses for women in order to keep themselves in employment. The dressing of a head for a fashionable function occupied three or four hours. With head-dresses of such enormous size it was essential for ladies to have hats to match, although sometimes a comparatively small hat was worn pinned firmly on top of the coiffure. Sometimes the hat was a part of the hairdressing, or, rather, the latter was so elaborate as to render a hat superfluous.

Bonnets of satin, taffeta, or linen were worn by women of all classes en négligé, i.e. on any occasion when full dress was not required, such as going to church or for a morning walk.

Long walking-sticks with gold or silver knobs were carried both by men and women, and the practice of wearing swords fell more and more into disuse, except among military men.

About the year 1778 a fashion arose of trimming the diagonal front edges of the overskirt with a frill of the same material as the flounces of the sleeves. The overskirt was sometimes puffed out with a stuffing of loosely crumpled paper which made a strange rustling noise when the wearer moved. The underskirt was richly ornamented either with horizontal gathers of its own material or with strips of lace, ribbon, or fur. The two skirts were frequently of contrasting colours or of lighter and deeper shades of the same colour. The skirt with *paniers*, before its final disappearance, was worn short, showing the shoes and the ankles, and, as always, a shorter skirt led to increased care for the neatness of shoes and stockings.

1770—1780

FROM the end of the seventeenth-seventies there is, quite suddenly, an enormous increase in the number of documents which may be consulted by the student of fashion. In a word, the fashion plate springs into being, and it is interesting to note that some of the earliest fashion plates were not concerned with the whole costume but with the method of dressing the hair. The fantastic hairdressing fashions of the decade made ladies all the more eager to be aware of the latest mode, and the engravers and publishers were not long in satisfying their curiosity.

A publication with the interesting title of *Souvenir a l'Anglaise et Recueil de Coëffures* appeared in Paris in 1778, and there was soon a rage for such aids to modernity on both sides of the Channel. The fashion paper was fairly launched and no doubt contributed largely to a more rapid changing of modes than had been customary or, indeed, possible earlier in the century. It is probable that the vogue for caricatures may have contributed to the same effect, for by exaggerating each fashion in turn and so tending to make it ridiculous, the growth of new fashions was stimulated. In England, however, the great growth of fashion plates belongs rather to the turn of the century than to the decade now under discussion.

Masculine hairdressing became neater and closer to the head, the three-cornered hat being very small and worn far forward, so that the brim came just above the eyes. Sleeves were sometimes extremely narrow, with a simple edge of lace protruding from the cuff. The formalised buttons and buttonholes, which had once had the genuine function of keeping the turned-back cuff in place, remained on the sleeve as decoration, just as they have remained to this day, sometimes as many as four, sometimes one, but never entirely absent. The *vestigial* element in dress is always large and is a proof of the extraordinary conservatism of fashion beneath all its apparent change.

1780

B Y the year 1780 the revived farthingale or hoop may be said to have disappeared, its place being taken by small pads or cushions fastened to the hips, and then by a single pad at the back. In fact, the eighteenth-century equivalent of the crinoline was followed by the eighteenth-century equivalent of the bustle, although neither of the names had as yet been invented. The recurrence of fashion is an attractive theory, but such recurrence obeys some peculiar rhythm of its own, so that prophecy becomes difficult if not impossible. There is, none the less, a certain parallelism between the course of fashion in the eighteenth and in the nineteenth centuries, even in small and seemingly unimportant details.

The fashion of embroidering men's coats all over their surface had now been abandoned. Even waistcoats were not so highly ornamented as they had been, the embroidery being now generally confined to the skirts, the pockets, and the buttonholes.

There was a reaction against high heels and a forecasting of the almost completely heelless shoes of the early nineteenth century. Improvements in the craft of shoemaking made all shoes much more comfortable, so that the use of house-slippers was abandoned. The long tongue of the upper disappeared almost completely.

For women, the large horizontal hat, usually worn at an engaging angle and adorned with ribbons or feathers, began to be fashionable in 1780, or soon afterwards. The material of these hats was straw or silk or some light foundation, and it was securely fastened to the coiffure with pins to prevent it from falling off. Even so it must have been no light task to manage the head-dress of the period in a high wind. Men were beginning to grow·tired of the universal *tricorne* and to cock their hats in a different way—straight up and down at the front and back, so that the two edges lay together. The hat thus treated was the ancestor of all the " Napoleonic " hats and of the cocked hats of modern admirals and generals.

1780—1785

ABOUT the year 1780 there was a wave of simplicity, not the real simplicity of the time of the Revolution, but a pseudo-pastoralism derived from the example of Marie Antoinette at the Trianon. There the ladies of the Court played at being shepherdesses and dressed their hair in "milkmaid" or "peasant" fashion, but dresses were no less costly for being pastoral or pseudo-pastoral. The influence of the country was more effective in England, where there was a real enthusiasm for rural life and where men, at least, wore clothes suitable for hard weather and boots adapted to the muddiness of the roads. Some women, finding a semi-masculine riding-dress becoming, adopted it for morning wear whether they intended to ride or not. The bodice was made in imitation of a man's coat and waistcoat with overlapping revers, and the skirt was full, but simple and without trimming. On ordinary dresses trimmings were abandoned in favour of ruches of muslin or lace, arranged in flounces and sewn to the edge of the dress. Gowns were worn rather long, and the white stockings were invisible. About the year 1783 there was a rage for decorating dresses with straw, even men's waistcoats being ribbed with it, and straw coats, called *paillasses*, were worn by women.

About 1780 hats began to be perched on the top of the high coiffures, with the result that the head-dress itself grew smaller to accommodate them. Hair was crimped and arranged in "hedgehog" fashion, puffed out from the face, and hats had to be very large in order to cover it without spoiling the effect. Some of the mob-caps of the period were almost as large as hoods and, indeed, resembled them very closely. On more formal hats there was a rage for ostrich feathers, a fashion immortalised by Gainsborough in his portrait of the Duchess of Devonshire.

1785—1790

TOWARDS the end of the 'eighties it became the fashion for women to wear a separate jacket-like garment called a *caraco*. This was close-fitting and made in a masculine style. Beneath it a tight-fitting dress was worn, bodice and skirt of the same material, the skirt contrasting with the *caraco*, which came more than ever to resemble a man's dress-coat. Sometimes the under-dress was without a bodice, a light corset being worn in its place, concealed by a kind of front or stomacher, made to resemble a man's waistcoat. This very masculine attire was sometimes worn with a large apron with pockets.

In winter *mantelets* were worn. These were short capes of silk occasionally edged with fur. When fitted with wide, half-length sleeves, the winter garment was called a *pelisse*.

From 1786 there was a fashion for beaver hats similar to those worn by men, but more richly trimmed.

The three-cornered hat may be said to have disappeared after the French Revolution. Shoe-buckles also fell out of fashion, being replaced by shoe-strings, although the growing use of boots rendered both unnecessary.

The heels of women's shoes were lower than they had been throughout the century, and the upper was more open, ending a couple of inches behind the toes. Shoes were more comfortably made, with the result that walking became more fashionable.

Swords, which had been worn throughout the century, disappeared about 1786, except with Court dress. About the same period, the wide skirts of men's coats gave place to long tails. Coats were double-breasted and very short in front, so as to reveal the waistcoat. In 1790 there was a temporary fashion for black coats, but the breeches and waistcoats remained brilliant in colour. Waistcoats and stockings were ornamented with vertical or horizontal stripes.

1780—1790

THE collars of men's coats, non-existent in the earlier part of the century, could be worn turned over in the modern fashion or else standing rigidly round the neck. The space between the neck and the collar was filled with a scarf wound several times round—the ancestor of the modern neck-tie. This neck-scarf was often of muslin, as its predecessor had been of cambric. Sleeves became still narrower and very long, so that little of the fine frills at the end of the shirt sleeve could be seen.

One of the fashionable methods of dressing the hair was to have two or three horizontal curls at the side and a little formal queue at the back. This mode has persisted, in a smaller, somewhat stylised form, in the barristers' wig of to-day, so that while the judge on the bench wears a wig dating in shape from the beginning of the eighteenth century, the wigs of counsel date from about 1780. State coachmen's wigs, worn by the coachmen of the nobility until the beginning of the twentieth century, date from the same period as those of barristers.

The typical head-dress of the seventeen-eighties for women tended to width, just as that of the 'seventies had tended to height. The effect was somewhat suggestive of the loose hair of a cavalier during the reign of Charles I. Over the hair large mob-caps could be worn, or else a broad-brimmed straw hat very simply trimmed. The general appearance could be charming. The hair, except on formal occasions, was worn without powder, but curling was essential if only to expand the hair to the required size. A kind of hood made of crape was very fashionable, and as the hair completely filled it, it was impossible to tell whether it was a hood or a cap. In winter hoods were edged with fur. Caps persisted for many years, and certain combinations of black and white lace remained as an old lady's head-dress in remote places for nearly a century.

1790

IN masculine attire the beginning of the seventeen-nineties marked the victory of English modes over French ones, and the beginning of a dominance which they have maintained ever since. The " European dress " established at the beginning of the century by the prestige of the French Court now gave place to a coat recognisably similar to that worn to-day in evening-dress.

The cut of the masculine coat had been fixed for so long that it must have seemed difficult, if not impossible, to change it. Ever since the evolution of coat and waistcoat at the end of the seventeenth century, the relationship of these two articles of attire had been constant. Now some genius adapted the double-breasted coat from the English riding-coat with its two rows of buttons, and two far-reaching consequences immediately followed, both caused by the necessity of keeping a double-breasted coat fastened if it is to preserve its fit. Had the coat been as long in front as formerly the wearer would have been considerably hampered in his movements, and the waistcoat—which had always provided an opportunity for the display of the wearer's taste—would have been totally concealed. Thus tailors began to experiment by cutting the front of the coat away. The period also witnessed an orgy of " revers," even waistcoats being provided with them, often of a colour contrasting with those of the coat.

As the waistcoat pockets were no longer easily accessible, it became the fashion to wear the watch in a front pocket of the breeches. Sometimes both front pockets carried a watch, with seals dangling down outside. The remote successors of these dangling seals were worn into the twentieth century, and may still occasionally be seen, but as the trousers have no front pockets, the " fob " is fastened to the braces.

E

1790—1795

DURING the early days of the Revolution in France, and most of all during " the Terror," it became positively dangerous to be seen in the streets of Paris in rich clothes. Not only was the cut plainer, but the materials also. Silks and satins disappeared, their place being taken by cotton, Indian print, and lawn. In England, there was less reason for change, not only because of the stability of the Government, but because the English gentleman with his country habits wore, by preference, clothes much less gaudy than those of his French counterpart. From one point of view, the Revolution was a victory for English fashions, even in France. The top-boots, the unembroidered coats, the stout breeches made for much hard wear in the saddle, passed from the country into the town, and men entered drawing-rooms in costumes more suited to the hunting-field. But Englishmen never adopted the extremely high and voluminous neck-clothes which in France actually rose to cover the chin and sometimes the mouth. A short bamboo cane or riding-whip replaced the long walking-stick of a few years before.

In women's costume, England almost entirely escaped the worst extravagances of the French *merveilleuses*, who went about the streets of Paris in a costume supposed to be Greek, consisting of one semi-transparent chemise-like dress with pink skin-tights worn underneath. The girdle was placed immediately under the breasts, and this fashion ·reached England towards the end of the century, when very high waists came into fashion. The rage for tall feathers also came from France—a little late, for they had been introduced by Marie Antoinette. It is curious to reflect that the custom of wearing two feathers upright in the hair, which began in this period, has lasted, in Court dress, until our own time.

1795—1800

IN the middle 'nineties, or, in extremely fashionable circles, just before, the short waist became the rage. The waist, in fact, slipped up to immediately below the breasts and remained there for about twenty years. The materials used for dresses were very thin, but unlike those employed in the days of *paniers*, they were neither used in great quantities nor elaborately patterned. Simplicity was pushed to the verge of indecency, although the transparent dresses worn in France were never popular in England. We have seen that at the beginning of the century English manufacturers were complaining of the importation of calicoes from India; now, owing chiefly to the invention by Arkwright of the spinning frame, the position was reversed, and the East India Company was driven to complain of the harm done to its import trade by the successful manufacture of British cottons and muslins.

The scantiness of dresses led to the popularity of large fur muffs and to the introduction of wraps, cashmere shawls, or sometimes mere handkerchiefs disposed like a fichu to protect the throat. A short, close-fitting coat with long sleeves, called the spencer, appeared about 1797.

In thin and unvoluminous dresses with no under-petticoats, women, at the end of the eighteenth century, found themselves confronted by a new problem—that of pockets. Their absence led to the invention of the reticule or handbag. It was much laughed at, but has survived several periods of eclipse, to become, in our own day, the most necessary accessory of female costume.

High-heeled shoes began to be discarded in favour of coloured slippers, made of satin for evening wear and of Morocco leather for day-time. They were extremely flimsy, for only eccentric young women, like Wordsworth's " dear child of Nature," went for long walks in the country.

1790—1800

IN 1795 Pitt imposed a tax on hair-powder, and so almost extinguished a fashion which was already on the wane, although true-blue Tories still continued to wear both wigs and hair-powder as a patriotic gesture, and to distinguish them from those who sympathised with the French Revolution. Political opinions sometimes decided the colour of a man's clothes. The Tory supporters of Pitt wore scarlet waistcoats, while the Whigs who supported Fox wore yellow. The partisans of Fox had also the very odd habit of carrying large red-fox muffs.

Sleeves became simpler than ever, the turned-back cuff being altogether abandoned, or else symbolised rather than imitated by a band of braid. The number of buttons worn on sleeves was also noticeably reduced.

About the year 1795 caps were discarded in fashionable circles in favour of bandeaux or fillets in supposed imitation of classical models. These fillets were made of muslin or of strips of coloured embroidery. Very few English women in these years of hostility to France followed the French fashion of having their hair cut short at the back and hanging in dishevelled locks over the face, *à la Titus*. A few may be noticed, however, particularly in the charming stipple engravings of Adam Buck.

From 1794 to 1797 there was a fashion for enormous ostrich plumes in the hair, sometimes two or three of different colours being worn together. The plainness of the dress of the period seemed to demand the wearing of jewellery, but as diamonds and other precious stones were temporarily out of fashion, semi-precious stones and corals were fashioned into cameos in imitation of the antique. Everything, in fact, was antique or pseudo-antique, and the century which began with the stiff splendour of the *Grand Siècle* ends in an orgy of the neo-classical.

  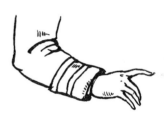